Samuel E. Solly

The Physician in Colorado

being the president's address to the Colorado State Medical Society

Samuel E. Solly

The Physician in Colorado
being the president's address to the Colorado State Medical Society

ISBN/EAN: 9783337870256

Printed in Europe, USA, Canada, Australia, Japan

Cover: Foto ©Andreas Hilbeck / pixelio.de

More available books at **www.hansebooks.com**

THE PHYSICIAN IN COLORADO

BEING THE

PRESIDENT'S ADDRESS

TO THE

Colorado State Medical Society,

–BY–

S. E. SOLLY, M. D.

THE PHYSICIAN IN COLORADO.

Gentlemen and Ladies—We are here to hold the eighteenth annual convention of our Society. Eighteen years is but a short period for a State Medical Society to have existed, but it has been long enough for us to grow from a weakly bantling, born by the praiseworthy efforts of a few Denver physicians, into an association of medical men from all parts of the State.

As the young maiden makes her debut in society when her eighteenth year is reached, so may we claim that, having quitted the sheltering arms of our kindly nurse Denver, and passed through the school of early trial and adversity, now make our debut among the ranks of the matured State societies of the country.

Even up to last year "the eternal want of pence which vexes public men," vexed ours. An empty exchequer made our time-honored Treasurer look almost middle-aged, and our Secretary was fast losing the buoyancy of youth. This year, thanks mainly to their energy, and the better appreciation of our merits by the brethren throughout the State, we rejoice in a full treasury and a greatly increased membership.

The literary menu that is offered for your discussion at this meeting promises, if hope tells not a flattering tale, and the bill of fare, as in past times, and as so often used that of our hotels, prove, "sweet to the eye, but in digestion sour," that we shall have a meeting as rich in medical interest as any that have gone before.

Another and important sign of our growth towards the wisdom becoming a State Society of the first rank, is the desire that has been generally manifested that we should so modify our by-laws, that we waste as little as possible of the time of our meetings upon the machinery of our organization, and save all we can for the real objects of our existence. We are an association primarily for the exchange of our medical thoughts and observations, and, secondarily, for the interchange of social amenities. Thus, by the first, we should add to our strength and armaments for the conquest of disease, and, by the second, knit up the ravelled sleeve of care, and, by rubbing off our angles in friendly intercourse, make it possible for future visitors to exclaim, on seeing us assembled: "How beautiful a thing it is to see the brethren dwelling together in unity."

It is, of course, essential for us, as an association, that we have a frame upon which to hang our work, as the skeleton is an essential part of the higher orders of beings. The most perfect specimens of development, however, are those in which the skeleton is most completely clothed, and in which its outlines are suggested, not shown. If we fail to spend our best hours in clothing our skeleton, and prefer rather to exhibit its nakedness and dispute over its anatomy, then, indeed, will our gatherings resound with nought but-the rattling of dry bones.

With a view of avoiding the fate just indicated, and for carrying out the legitimate objects of our association, as before expressed, your Committee on By-Laws was appointed, with instructions to prepare a scheme, and this will be presented to you in due course. Whether the plans suggested are the best to accomplish the end in view, is not here my place to discuss, but I congratulate you upon the distinct advance towards an ideal which the ventilating of this question shows.

In attending the first meeting of the Association of American Physicians, I was much impressed with these words from the lips of Dr. Delafield, the President, which seem to me to epitomize the spirit that should animate all scientific medical bodies, allowing, of course, wider latitude in certain directions in a general society such as ours, than is needed in one of the limited aims and membership that he was addressing. What he said seems largely applicable to our own wants and needs, and thus he spake: "We want an association in which there will be no medical politics and no medical ethics; an association in which no one will care who are the officers, and who are not; in which we will not ask from what part of the country a man comes, but whether he has done good work, and will do more; whether he has something to say worth hearing, and can say it. We want an association composed of members, each one of whom is able to contribute something real to the common stock of knowledge, and where he, who reads such a contribution, feels sure of a discriminating audience."

Passing from these considerations of ourselves as a collective body, I would beg your attention for a brief space, to spend some thought upon the unit which goes to make this body corporate—that is, let us discuss the physician in Colorado; the man himself, his surroundings, and his work.

As yet I believe we can claim no native physician, omitting, perhaps, the family physician of the melancholy Ute, who, not being a regular graduate, cannot be admitted a member of our State Society, though our legislators, with more of charity than discretion, would doubtless enroll him on their register as a legally qualified practitioner under the ten years' clause, providing he produce for them the most essential qualification of a five-dollar bill.

> "Let observation, with extended view,
> Survey mankind from China to Peru."

And it can then, and only then, take in the varied nativity of our Colorado doctors.

We came hither from living, and most of us from practicing, under very different conditions, both as regards people and climate, to those among which we now pursue our art. Our collective experience should therefore give us so wide a variety of observations of disease as to furnish us with all the material needed, from which to extract and formulate the typical and essential qualities of any given malady.

Thus, having gained a knowledge of what constitutes a special disease, we can then observe the modifications in its manifestations that are produced by our peculiar climatic and racial conditions, so as to measure their true effect and value.

Owing to our wide collective experience, we stand more in the position of a society like the American Medical Association than that of a society of a single State.

Having indicated that we, of all practitioners of medicine, should be especially able, with each other's aid, to define what are the essentials of each wide-spread specific disease, let us pass on to consider our surroundings.

Here, gentlemen, tempting as is the old familiar path, I will not dilate at length upon our climate, but will briefly refer to its salient features. The elevations above sea level, at which we practice, range from four to ten thousand feet; the configuration of the ground, generally undulating, consists of plateau, mountain, valley, and mountain side; the soil is mostly dry, light and porous or rocky, and innocent of malaria; the vegetation scanty; an absence of and a great distance from large bodies of water; pure water, derived from widely scattered mountain streams and a few small lakes; a small relative humidity, ranging from 10° to 46°, and an actual humidity averaging about ——; a rain and snow fall which, combined, rarely exceeds fifteen inches a year; an almost constant movement of atmosphere, though, even on the plains, the total annual movement and velocity is decidedly less than at most of the cities of the states near either ocean or the great lakes; a high temperature in the sun and a low one in the shade and at night, especially marked in winter; considerable thermometric range and rapid change: brilliant sunlight and an almost

unrivaled proportion of clear and fair days; an especially
pure air, as shown by the quick healing of wounds.
These, briefly, are our climatic peculiarities.

To touch upon the racial features of our clients, we
may say, omitting the Utes, with few exceptions, "they
are not to the manor born," but like ourselves, come from
the four quarters of the globe. They bring with them
their racial and local peculiarities and habits, which,
although partly modified in all by this especial change of
surroundings, yet give each a considerable variation in
personal characteristics from one another and from pa-
tients taken from a people who have, and whose parents
have, lived always in the same climate.

The food also with which they are nourished is cosmo-
politan in character, being gathered in from all parts of
the world, to a greater extent than is common in most
countries. Thus much of our surroundings, our people and ourselves. Now let us pass on to consider, as time
permits, the features of the work in science's cause that
lies ready to our hand.

To add to the stock of facts concerning the influence of
the Colorado climate upon the type and progress of disease, and to intelligently guide those who desire to come
to us to regain the lost boon of health, is outside the work
that falls to each of us in our ordinary avocation as physicians—the duty that we owe to science.

First, we need to ascertain, as far as is permitted us, by
our experience elsewhere, by comparison among ourselves of those experiences, and by the reading of recorded
facts and observations, what are the essential features of a
typical specimen of the disease we wish to study.

Next, by recording, first by ourselves and then together,
our observations upon the action of disease in Colorado,
accumulate facts for comparison. Having thus established the premises that there are certain defined modifications of disease created by the climate, then let us search
for the causes of these variations. Thus having defined
the disease, first in its essential, and then in its modified
form, we pass to the patient and his environments.

Taking the patient as an individual, it behooves us to
classify him according to his temperament and type of
physique, and here we can search back, if leisure allows,
into the especial characteristics of the race from which
he sprang and the especial influences of the climate from
whence he came to Colorado.

The patient's environments should then claim our consideration. Knowing the general climatic and meteoro-
logic conditions of his present abode, we can proceed to
study what is known of the effects of the various ele-

ments that go to make the climate, upon the healthy human body, separately and in combination, and the physical and physiological reasons for them. Having thus constructed a frame of established scientific fact, we proceed to add to it the empirical knowledge recorded by observers in other climates and the observations we ourselves make in this climate, separately and in combination. Thus, having formed a body composed of scientific and empirical fact, we are justified in putting forth our theories which, when attached to such a body, are useful antennæ, to feel the way along the path of truth, but which, when out of proportion to the body of fact and improperly attached to it, become useless members, fit only for amputation by the knife of truth.

The knowledge of scientific climatalogy among the profession generally is very slight; they decide upon the merits of a climate usually from the general assertions of physicians practicing in certain localities or from their experience in one or two instances where the climate has been tried, and they do not study or draw their conclusions from the underlying facts of climatology, which alone give the necessary basis for forming a reasonable estimate of the probable effects of a given climate upon a given case.

Meteorology also, in connection with prevailing or passing types of disease, is too little studied in this country. I trust all members of this Society will join the State Meteorological Association, and will take observations themselves or aid in their being taken in their respective localities, so that our knowledge of the climate and weather over the whole of the inhabited portions of Colorado may be complete, and after a series of years we may present to the profession indubitable facts concerning the meteorology of these elevated regions, such as will be of inestimable value. In this connection I may mention that, as the government have decided, from motives of economy, to abandon their signal station upon Pike's Peak, we have formed a society in this town with the view of carrying on the observations and other work, both meteorological and physiological, whereby we hope in time to solve such problems as the cause of mountain sickness and others, the explanation of which are now only speculative. Also by means of self-recording instruments in our college observatory, we are beginning to demonstrate facts which will no doubt prove valuable to us as physicians.

In studying the influence of the Colorado climate upon pathological conditions, we need first to acquaint ourselves with the outlines of what is known about the geographical distribution of disease. Knowing the range of temperature, latitude and average humidity of a climate, we can roughly predict the chief diseases that will be found among its residents. In hot countries, affections of the bowels and liver and malarial fevers are most common ; in cold climates, catarrhal affections of the respiratory tract, and in temperate, tubercular and renal diseases are most frequent. These facts have been established largely from statistics made from observations upon the health of the British troops stationed in various portions of the globe. The modifying influence of altitude, considered as a separate factor, has, however, been so far too little studied.

In estimating and recording the effects of this climate upon the various organs, it is necessary to take into consideration the race and temperament of the individual, and these will probably generally explain apparent contradictions. Take the liver, for example. It is frequently asserted, on the one hand, that this climate causes billiousness, and, on the other, that it relieves it. I have formed the impression that what is called a bilious person, one who at home frequently exhibited signs of functional hepatic irregularities is, while resident in this climate, less subject to them, and his skin is apt to lose its yellowish tinge. Whilst with persons of a sanguine or nervous temperament, in whom such attacks had previously been rare are, whilst here, not uncommonly subject to such disorders. The explanation for this assumed fact appears to me to be, briefly, as follows : In the individual of bilious temperament the cause of their derangement was mainly from lack of sufficient stimulus to the liver through its circulatory or nervous supply, or both, and that the acknowledged activity of these two systems, induced by the climate, was the cause of the better working of the organ. In the individuals of sanguine or nervous temperament the circulatory and nervous supply of their livers being already sufficiently active, the climatic stimulus would come in excess and induce a condition in which slight exciting causes would readily give rise to active congestion of the liver and subsequent derangement. Neither place nor time permits me to discuss the details of the various interesting problems presented to us for solution. I will, therefore, only suggest the outlines of some of the studies that seem proper for us individually and collectively to pursue.

Conceding as a generality, as undoubtedly we all assembled here do, that this climate tends to arrest and sometimes to cure phthisis. And omitting from our consideration those cases in which death already holds the winning cards, and leaving out, also, those who although coming hither

nominally to fight a battle for their life, put wisdom on
one side and by their neglect and deliberate folly give
from the first, victory to the foe; and taking thought only
of those in whom the balance appears to be still in their
favor, and who do their best to win. Why is it that some
fail and others gain? What are the pathological conditions
of phthisis which this climate is best adapted to remove
or arrest? And what are those for which a different air is
indicated? I have, as no doubt have most of you, formed
opinions on this subject, and an interchange of our experiences would probably add to our empirical knowledge.
It is, however, through a study beginning with climatology and physiology, and crowned by our experience, that
we can pick up the clue that will enable us to formulate
such crude ideas into a scheme whereby we can predict
with fair accuracy what cases are or are not suitable for
treatment here.

The diseased lung that needs a stimulus would appear
to be benefited, and the one that requires rest, harmed.

There is an interesting field open to us in the study of
the influence of Colorado upon catarrhs, and especially
on those of the respiratory tract. I think such inquiries
as I have suggested will show us how to reconcile the two
opposite opinions, so often expressed, that this country is
and is not good for nasal catarrh. The dry air probably
acts as a stimulus to the mucous membrane, calling forth
excessive exosmosis from its glands, and causing such
rapid evaporation that the secretion loses its water and
remains hard and dry upon its surface, instead of pro-
tecting it with a little lubricating fluid. Such, doubtless, is the effect upon the already hyperæmic mucous
membrane, and temporarily more or less the effect upon
the normal one. When, on the other hand, there is an
anæmic mucous membrane, with a passively weeping surface, the hyperæmia induced by the dry air, probably
works a cure by its stimulating quality. Going further
down the respiratory tract to the larynx, the same contradictions appear, and their explanation can apparently be
sought successfully along the same lines. And further
yet, it would appear as if the climatic influence upon catarrhs of the bronchi could be decided upon the same
principles, and perhaps, too, the phthisis which seems to
originate and be closely connected with capillary bron-
chitis. When, however, we proceed further and consider
primary affections of the parenchyma and alveoli of the
lungs themselves, our line of investigation clearly needs
changing.

Putting on one side, for the sake of argument, the di-
rect phenomena of tubercle and its accompanying and

apparently causitive bacillus, let us glance at the condition of the pulmonary circulation as influenced by the climate in pathological states. If the state is one of anœmia, or of passive congestion, the increased activity of the lungs, caused by the rarefaction and dryness, would tend to remove it. On the other hand, should the condition be that of hyperæmia, active congestion or inflammation, the undue exercise would surely increase it.

Touching thus suggestively upon these topics, and not attempting to treat them exhaustively, let me, before closing, refer to fever accompanying pulmonary affections. The effect of the climate is apparently to increase inflammation when present, for a time at least, and consequently to also increase the accompanying fever. There are also grounds for the belief that pneumonia increases in severity and frequency with altitude, allowing comparisons only between cases in which the underlying conditions of general health and the hygenic surroundings are on a par. In cases of phthisis, however, which come here with fever, after a brief temporary increase, the fever usually falls, where the climate agrees. This apparent contradiction can no doubt be explained by going to the underlying principles of climatology, as well as to the pathology of the disease.

It being so true, that life is short and art is long, I must leave these and other interesting problems for our future solution by combined effort. My object here is to stimulate inquiry, not to record it, and to point out that we have all of us a stewardship of which we should give account. That we should each of us endeavor in our turn to unravel the tangled web of truth and fiction that is wrapped around these questions. That the way to do it, so our work may last, is to start from a scientific basis, and then when the many facts cross and recross each other in the path of our investigations, call in our art and experience to aid our conclusions; for ours is an art, though it should always spring from the soil of science, so let us reverence in due regard honest observation.

"For old experience doth attain,
To something of prophetic strain."

www.ingramcontent.com/pod-product-compliance
Lightning Source LLC
Chambersburg PA
CBHW021622290326
41931CB00047B/1444